Using Your Words

Using Your Words

Poems by

Laura Rogerson Moore

Kelsay Books

© 2017 Laura Rogerson Moore. All rights reserved. This material may not be reproduced in any form, published, reprinted, recorded, performed, broadcast, rewritten or redistributed without the explicit permission of Laura Rogerson Moore. All such actions are strictly prohibited by law.

Cover: *Water Is Love*
by Katherine Rogerson Moore,
oil on canvas

ISBN: 13- 978-1-947465-34-3

Kelsay Books
Aldrich Press
www.kelsaybooks.com

*With gratitude for my mothers and my daughters
and for RCM*

Contents

Girl in the Mirror	9
Without Saying	10
Everything Leaves	11
Darkness Not Darkness	12
Feathers in a Jar	13
Water is Love	14
As It Is	15
Homemade	17
Everything You Need to Know	18
An Owl, a Field, a Moon	19
How Else	20
Word World	21
Toward Goodness	22
The Pot of Gold	23
Somewhere Elsewhere	24
Within Without	25
Undoing	26
Quiet Places	27
After All, Always Somewhere	28
Ever Mindful of the Needs of Others	29
Non-Speaking Role	30
Hard to Get	31
Same Thing Twice	32
What You Were Told	34
Bien	36
What He Said	37
The Right Amount	38
Good Girl	39
What You Mean	40
Resolution	41
Inside Out	42

Lady Bug, Lady Bug	43
The Words for Things	44
Giving It Up	46
Golden Rod	47
Time Telling	48
Not Vast but Wilderness	49
Ho Jo and Flo	50
Won't You Be	52
Fly Away Home	53
Sonnet for Freshman English	54
Between the Window and the Door	55
Not as Much	56
Shbag	57
Saturday, After Midnight	58
No Cause, No Cause	60
Baby Teeth	61
Using Your Words	62
Being Pleased	63
The Various Shapes of Leaves	64
Becoming	65
Unbecoming	66
The Forgiveness Bowl	67
Learning How to Tie	68
Burden of the Past	69
Blue Flight, Blue Bird, Sky	70
At Its Best	71
Housekeeping	72
Having It All	73
The Knot	74
The Rest of It	75
The Dragonfly	76

About the Author

Girl in the Mirror

And after all, you refuse to see the gains,
the losses, blemishes and dark circles,
lack and then abundance of sleep, only
catching glimpses between semesters, long
weekends, home from college for just a little
while until you and Randall return from
a trip unexpectedly early to find

mixing bowls in the sink, a half-eaten
sheet cake in the fridge, take-out boxes in
the trash, three empty mint chocolate chip
ice cream cartons – the lights will be on, but
Louisiana won't be home, and you

remember standing over the sink, chewing
and not swallowing spoonful after spoonful,
spitting the spoils down the drain; the way it
began – hard-boiled eggs and admiration –
a little, less, nothing – Dexatrim, black
coffee, nicotine unfiltered, late nights,
long walks, smaller jeans – until you weren't

even looking at a girl in the mirror,
refusing and refusing and refusing –
your whole body a strength that terrified –
a hollow inside yourself, a hungry
cave of loneliness, past appetite, taste;
powerful in choosing to live this way –

one emptiness and all the removals –
days your life won't retrieve. You remember
how you were, and you are sore afraid.

Without Saying

You snuck out from time out,
ran when you were called.
When Daddy came home,
you got what you deserved.

"I hope you have a daughter
just like you," Mum hollered
or snarled when she couldn't
catch you – dryer running,
babies crying, dishes in the sink,
supper on the stove.

Sometimes as you were lying
on your bed and she was hearing
your prayers, hardly

listening, distracted
by the peace
of her own quiet

body, she summoned
everything you'd ever need to know
without saying a word.

Everything Leaves

Outside, above the barn, maple
leaves – late turners – drop and twirl

down. Once you thought you couldn't live
without Tate. Without Mum, Daddy once
you couldn't either. Everything

leaves. Your daughter, the bowl
in which you bore her, the weight of her
becoming. How did it happen?

A shredding of clouds
moving away from themselves,
becoming more than one
cloud, silently? The tearing

of a seam – front and back?
Is it a matter of division
or differentiation?

Repetition or rhyme?

Darkness Not Darkness

Each morning, Weezie asks if you came
into her room last night. She swears
she saw you there, and you remember

waking, listening, paddling your breath
toward that other sleep in that other room.

Louisiana keeps reminding you
of solitudes you've always known.
All the lonesome hours repeating

the questions – darkness
not darkness, separating

light. No one knew what to do
and none to tell you either. The long
corridors of sadness – to and fro

you roamed them – hours
in your room, late late

nights in front of classic movies on
the TV, a smuggled glass of Daddy's
whiskey, a muffled stumble up the stairs.

Feathers in a Jar

Some things are just meant
to be borne – the boat

on the water, your shadows
on the nearest shore, her feet

in your shoes, sunlight
on your hair, breath

in your bodies – feathers
in a jar. "All this pain,

how insane – so much
to gain. Who knows when

I'll be back this way again."
Weezie sings what she writes,

and you cannot accept
responsibility for her grief,

nor can you
minister to her joy.

Over the surface of the pond
so many swallows

perform their exquisite
choreography.

Water is Love

You used to read Louisiana
a story in which a father tells
his son, "You must always have a quiet

place inside your head, for if you have no quiet
place, you will have nowhere to go." To which
she replied, "Water is love." So, you went

to find it in the hollows of fallen
leaves, wheel ruts rainbowed with oil, twinkling on
bits of cellophane, broken glass. Weezie

used to get sick on airplanes, but in her dreams
she flew, and she would tell you of the beating
things that pulled her shoulder blades, shrugging at

their memory. Once, you, too, flew in a dream,
right after choosing to do what Mum
had done – diapers, meals, essays, class,

a room to call your own. "Mumma, when I grow
up, I will be a line," Weezie used to
say. And when you asked her what she was right

then, "A circle." You shared a pulse once.
Your hearts kept time.

As It Is

While the pond reflects
the sky, rim to rim,

words you've never said
and always used

feather the nests of Weezie's
songs, flapping, flying,

through an open window,
into a sky unclouded

with sorrow, joy, and
promises no one's made –

so many words to
occupy your mind.

If it said *don't*, you did.
Now no one bothers

to remind you of
your little trespasses.

"Words unspoken
won't make you broken.

Pack up your prize
and go, unwise,

to love unduly
in ways which truly

loosen all
that's been untied."

Homemade

No one sat with you at lunch or on the bus; no one
played with you at recess. You rolled your knee socks
down, folded your waistband over once, then twice.

You tried to grow your bangs. "You shouldn't stoop to
their level," Mum would say. And when you whined that was
what the other girls got to do, "You're not them."

Into the night, the sewing machine whirred upstairs,
fabric splitting and bending, tucking and folding
to form the way to be a girl who used to canter, claw,

bellow, guffaw, blast, hurtle past, stand up
to pee in the bushes, barefoot, open-mouthed,
at the top of your lungs, at the top of a tree,

in the rafters of the barn. The pins she forgot
in the seams sometimes stuck you, a meanness
of which you were learning the world was full.

Everything You Need to Know

Beyond the places where your clothing ends, the tiny red
dots of their spines stuttered across your naked skin.

The boys hurled the casings at you, and the chestnut tree
above, to which you were tied, from which the chestnuts fell

in their horrid shells, dappled their fear and shame
with sunlight that squinted between its plate-sized leaves.

You used to be a boy, too.

The other girls tottered back to watch no one rescue you,
their siren-screams clenched within their whispering hands.

At home Mum would be welcoming Daddy, who'd have spent
the day at the hospital, consoling the sick and dying –

All Things Considered on the radio and supper in the oven.
"I'm done," she'd say, and with that, desert the kitchen,

her feet scolding every stair all the way to her room.
And your brothers?

Somewhere in the woods until the five o'clock whistle,
never even near, not looking to be found.

An Owl, a Field, a Moon

A soundless silhouette stands

against your waking, and you roll over,
making room for her in your wide dark
bed. Weezie followed you all day – a shadow
you bumped into when you changed course too

fast – not eating, not

speaking, studying the ceiling fan's returning
of the air it would return again in just a little while.
She can't go back, no matter how. Instead,

this march of minutes, this climb
of light up walls and down again,
a pot roast simmering, a pumpkin pie
cooling, and Randall in the yard,
working on his truck as shadows
lengthen on another close of day.

How you used to fight with love,
or for it – a cup whose only use

its emptiness.

Walking the dogs into the woods, you
and Weezie see an owl you follow
beyond the trees, across a field, wide and
hollow with sinking light, as overhead

a newly waxing moon mutely blooms.

How Else

How to tease
apart her beginning,
your ending –

her becoming a rebuke
or homage? Some
response? Or will

none of it matter,
all of a mother's life
a locking up and letting go?

Mum kept saying
she hoped you'd have a daughter
just like you

as she slammed the door
to your room before
she turned the key.

How else could you
love each other?
A rock won't float,

yet waters wash it
clean. Each word can mean
so many things. Describe

this life.

Word World

Spell your own name.
Color inside the lines.
Remember the letters
in the order that makes

a word

you can read to know
the sentence that tells
the story that goes with
the pictures that order

a world

which marches left
to right, black
on white – naming
and leaving the rest

unsaid.

When Daddy read you
the story, you rested your head
on his chest so you heard the words
inside and out, both,

at once

seeing it with the clarity
of its nouns, the strength
of its verbs; loving it
with the pronouns'

abandon.

Toward Goodness

Imagining all you
had given up in a heap
of longing,

imagining a flight
toward goodness,

imagining yourself
so poor your misery had no need
of explanation,

you gave your word –
once Daddy explained
that it was not one word

you had that was yours to give –
and the giving was winged,
sky-blue, sleepy-eyed

with fluffiness and dead-foot
numb, as if you had been
kneeling far too long.

"Naughty," Mum used to tell him,
once upon a time. That word
squeezed under your door –

one syllable, then the next –

scooting into your lap
where you patted it
so it wouldn't bite.

The Pot of Gold

After the registrar, bursar, doctor,
therapist, pharmacy, you

drive around, choosing old back roads,
ways you used to go, especially in the rain,

past shining fields, beneath the dripping trees –
tires kissing, puddles slapping.

When you see a rainbow, you remind Weezie
how she once asked if you could drive to its end.

How does it happen – the same thing, twice?
What is it you've not done?

Too often, you weren't able to slow down.
In your hurry, grabbing, grim-faced –

all you had to do, both of you, and time
no longer passing, just decisions made

in empty rooms with doors flung wide
by someone you didn't even know was there.

Somewhere Elsewhere

Most Sundays after church, you all piled
in the car and drove to Pop's. Even
if you didn't listen to the words
themselves, you understood what everyone
was saying – appearances, money, people's
habits – your mother and Mrs. Fisk in
the kitchen, your father and her father in
the den, you and the boys outside on
the jungle gym, except when it rained.

As you drove home the back way, you listened to
NPR, the ball game, your brothers
falling asleep while you felt sick and
Mum complained about the expectations –
teas and altar guild, the Junior League – the
labels – minister's wife, housewife,
mother, daughter, returning student,
feminist, having it all. Daddy told her
they're all just words; she'd made her choices
and to forget about it; go to school;
finish her degree; the world would change
regardless of whether she could change it. While

you stirred up supper – scrambled eggs and toast –
Mum stomped upstairs to write another
paper, so the next day, she could drive away
to somewhere else, where only she could be, and
you wouldn't be able to tell her all
she needed to know. Though words spilled out
before you'd even thought what you had to say,
as if there'd always be enough to go
around, what you told her didn't make her stay,
and Daddy had to leave the room.

Within Without

Told to learn
to live without,

you had to learn
to live within.

So solitude
collapses time,

which holds its breath
and swims with eyes

wide open in this
breathless world.

You will not
remember how

you passed it,
only that you could.

Undoing

You asked her if you could
try it and she let you –
home late from class and
finished eating the plate of
food you'd saved for her.

It hurt, but not as much
as the first time, which you knew
you'd eventually end up
telling her about (behind
the hardware store with the new
girls from across the street
and their dad's Kools).

Mum scribbled the wine
around in her glass. "Fuck it,"
her mouth scrawled. She paused
at the sink, accusing
her own dirty dishes,
then undid everything

with a laugh, smudged with the smoke
that smeared her open mouth,
pale and grey and dissipating,
as if you both could pretend
nothing was really there.

Quiet Places

You bathed them, tucked them to bed,
gathered their shirts, underpants,
those dirty socks, lining their shoes
along the wall, so when your brothers
woke with feverish fears, unhindered,
they would wade the dark to you.

At break of day
you found them floating
at the foot of your dreams –

three little boys

who ate berries off the bush,
wiped their collars cross their mouths,
jumped feet-first into the river,

sprawled upon its bank
while overhead the soundless clouds
soft-shoed from horizon

to horizon.

After All, Always Somewhere

Why would you rush so,
when love seems to be
a matter of time, which is,

really, all you had
to lose? While Mum was
busy with reinvention, she made

her little bargain with you
as hours carried minutes
day after day into the curve

of thought, one place
to dwell.

        Were you not
all striving, tuned to these

years – no map, no compass –
your own North Star your lives
thus far? After all, your choices

became Weezie's choices, too.
After all, always, somewhere,
the sun is rising into more

time. And after all, you cannot
lead anyone else into a dream.
Nor should you try to follow.

Ever Mindful of the Needs of Others

After you washed the dishes, you wandered
into the back yard – cold air and stars back
of some coming weather. Across the street,
Rosie and Sarah's house hid in the dark.

You thought of sleeping over, songs playing
on the radio – words to know by, "A score
for your life?" Daddy used to ask, never
having really listened. The week before,

at church supper, you'd hung your head to hear
your father's blessing, careful not to touch
elbows with the boys on either side of
you. Hot and shivery – when Mum asked, you'd

tried to sit up straight and smile. Out the window,
as the blue swallowed a bird, everything
green boasted into silence you'd have sworn
you could hear. No boys ever noticed you

until they did. Once, on the stairs, trailing
your fingers on the rail, another hand
perched on yours and coated you in skin.

Non-Speaking Role

In English Comp. Sarah and Rosie spoke
without raising their hands while you waited
for a boy to finish any sentence
you began and earned the praises they deserved.
You'd never paid attention, didn't know

any of the rules, but Rosie said she
liked the freshman captain, and he liked her;
so, you watched the football games. Because
you could not throw a ball, you auditioned for
the play and were cast an extra. He

was set to play the lead. At rehearsals
you sat beside him, and he spoke, just of Rosie,
the way Rosie spoke of him, shivering
on the sidelines, in the autumn air, waiting
for the boys to line up, get hit, line up,

to get hit again. At the girls' games, Rosie
shot, and Sarah saved, and Tate leaned against
the wall on which you leaned. When he spoke of
Rosie, you listened carefully as he
told you what he thought she'd want to hear.

Hard to Get

Tossing the day inside out, Mum
served leftover birthday cake
for breakfast, or butterscotch sundaes,
rehashing old news, favoring you,
your triumphs, over any of your friends',
words falling from her mouth
like frogs and stones. And the boys?

"Keep 'em guessing; string 'em along."

You swallowed spoonful after spoonful,
licking the bowl when you were through.
When you rose to clear the table,
she'd give your bottom a little pat.

"Stand up straight. Tuck that in."

If Mum was home for supper and
Daddy was away, you could get
her laughing hard enough to make her drool,
and no one got sent to the kitchen
to eat his supper all alone.

Same Thing Twice

Saving her secrets for songs,
Weezie wrote in metaphors to make
out truths you can only imagine

now – pages filled with words
that hum to tunes no one else
can hear, let alone sing along to –

numbered questions, answer keys,
the main idea, its evidence,
the root, the graph, the sine,

the dead of night, the early day,
the practice for the game,
the party at some summer house,

the loveless boys who ask for love,
the girls who tell them how,
the booze, the bodies

bumping in the night,
the eyes, the mouths
made up, and clothes

no one belongs to. Oh, you
wild adventurous girl who laughed
too loudly, who slammed the door,

who shook the rafters
with your footfall on the stair,
who cried for shame,

who pulled the shade,
who sometimes wished
that you were dead.

What You Were Told

Sarah told you about Rosie and Rosie
told you about Sarah and both of them
told you about Tate and you wondered what
they told each other about you. Before

the school dance, Sarah and Rosie would drink
vodka and Tang from shampoo bottles
they kept on their dresser. They'd sneak out after
curfew and meet down in the woods behind

the hardware store. For your sixteenth birthday
they invited you to smoke some pot with them,
and at first you didn't feel a thing until
you couldn't stop feeling everything.

"We don't like what you're becoming," Daddy
told you. You were finally beginning
to understand becoming was something
you could change, like a dress; only he gave you

words like *integrity* and *solitude*.
He told you to take care of yourself, that you
were all you had, and following the crowd
would leave you alone in the end. He gave

you more words – *compromise*, *superficiality*
and *meanness*. You thought about your place upon
the circle, the words they whispered there,
the people those words were for, the ways you

leaned in to learn them. He never said *bitch*,
but you knew that was what he meant. You knew
Mum didn't disagree, and you didn't
yet know how you'd bear the weight of their

expectations as a blade of grass does
a bird, because a bird is meant to fly.
"You are so much better than that," he told
you. "You deserve so much more," Mum said. And

when you didn't get a prize at prize day,
they spent the car ride home telling you why
you should have. You looked out at the world rushing
past; you thought about the fortress of

aloneness you kept constructing, but you
still didn't know there were words for it.
All you had was *perfection*. Rosie and
Sarah kept doing what they did. Tate went off

with them, and you were uninvolved. You
got so angry and such headaches. And then
you got caught talking in the library.
You tried to do what you were told. You came

home for supper. You did the dishes after.

Bien

"You could be a native speaker," Madame
cried. "Memorize more vocabulary."

You mimicked others easily and learned
the words for things they expected you to
say. Late at night, alone in your room, the windows
stared back at you, black-eyed six over six,
a world behind that glassy look. The words
you learned were meant for things you'd never use.
The praise you earned you needed to deserve.
You could only weep when you couldn't

understand. Mum would come in to say good
night before she went to bed, and Daddy
left the light on in the hall. You were

earning choices, you knew. You'd have more because
you'd worked so hard and learned what you were supposed
to learn. One day when Tate was wearing your
favorite sweater and you didn't get to eat
your lunch with him because you had to go to
extra help in math instead, you sobbed for
twenty minutes in a bathroom stall.
Later, when you talked to him before his football
practice, he told you he had a history
paper to write that night, and you almost
figured out what to say to that, but then

you didn't, remembering it's better
to say nothing if you've nothing nice

to say at all.

What He Said

You'd take very quiet
walks along the river,
whenever you could

get away. "I forget
how nice your hands
feel," he would say. "Your hair

looks beautiful
that long." At night
if he called,

Daddy almost always
scared him off. You never
talked for long.

The Right Amount

For what? you want to ask her –
sex and those things men do?
Money, math, and managing?

Cars and driving, finding your way?
The girls whose friendships
turn, like milk, then curdle and sour?

Leaving your parents in the house
of worship they have built themselves
and marrying a man who will redeem you?

What's the right amount for raising

a girl? Just enough to starve her,
leave her lonesome, wishing
she were dead? "That's what my mother

lived long enough to say to me," Mum says.
Under the table, Randall reaches
for your hand, while outside Weezie

wanders barefoot by the pond whose fearless
waters fill its bowl with echoes
of a weightless true and empty sky.

Good Girl

Springtime and the peepers cry
out for each other,

and the trail is darker than
the darkening air,

and from up ahead of you, shirt-tails flying,
bare feet pumping the pedals

as she disappears into
the sightless night,

Louisiana's voice drifts down,
"I had a dream last night

that I could lick myself all
over, like a dog, until

I became invisible."
And though you cannot see

her, you know that
voice, how it has changed her

face as she starts to sing,
"Cause I'm free,

I'm free falling."

What You Mean

The moon is only visible
because the sun
undoes its darkness.

Some loves you choose.
Some love chooses you.
Call it love and wish it love

when what you mean is
something else – a knot
you can't untie.

Unlatch and open.

A thousand thoughts fly out,
white with hope of light
that may not break.

Resolution

Mrs. Goodnough leaned out
the car window. "Isn't it

beautiful?" And you saw it was —
the pink sky and the snowy

trees. You decided to walk
as far as the town shed, the snow

wrapping your feet, the moon
yellow-white wrapped

in rings. A first star appeared,
and a fox looked at you across

a field, and you listened to
the snow sitting in the trees

and resolved for this new
year you would be sweeter.

Inside Out

Words flew, fierce
with righteous rage –
everything handed

to her and always
some man there
to help her out,

Pop's little motherless
daughter, the minister's
outrageous wife –

nothing ever enough, nothing
earned, and nothing let go.
This frantic bird bashed

its wings against your skull,
a feathery noise, inside out.
You'd thrown your brothers'

lacrosse ball through a window
because Daddy told you it was too late
to go over to Rosie and Sarah's.

And then the toilet tank lid
broke in two because Mum wouldn't
let you use the phone.

Lady Bug, Lady Bug

When she was
little, Weezie
caught lady bugs,

trapping them in jars,
petting them until
they died.

"He's gone to sleep,
Mumma," she'd tell you.
You taught her to sing

that old song, "Lady
Bug, Lady Bug, fly
away home. Your

house is on fire,
and your children –
they will burn."

The Words for Things

Eating compulsively, hating being
alone and being with people, never
sure what you were doing, worrying

you'd say something, wishing you were doing
something else, dancing alone in your room
with all the lights turned out. Mum told you that

you shouldn't stay on the wait list, that you
shouldn't follow Rosie, Sarah, and Tate
to college; they couldn't be trusted; you

poured too much into them and lost yourself,
got nothing in return. You were too good
for them. They didn't love you back enough,

and besides, you should create your own self,
find your own school, do what she did, on your
own, what she wished her mother had been there

to tell her she ought to do; that you were
a very demanding child, always had
been. She tried to paste you back together

by saying this was because you were so
gifted. You went up to your room and tried
to read and thought, suddenly, you might jump

out the window or throw up or press your
body against your cold white wall. You were
bad, full of badness. So much anger

jealousy, self-loathing made you do
or think of doing things that were so bad. As
a child, you were bad. As a girl, you'd learned

to bury the worst, but still so many
things wouldn't stay put, couldn't be told. You
wouldn't even look at yourself. You'd learned

to pretend. You could act good very well.
Sometimes you even wrote down your lies, so
what you wanted to believe could come nearer

being true. The worst thing about going
deeper was finding how bad you really
were. The worst thing about growing up was

going deeper, having deeper to go.
Besides, it was hard to find the words, once
you went there, to tell yourself what you'd found.

Giving It Up

There were times when you actually considered it.
Three times, actually. Once, when you'd found out
your math teacher saw you looking at Rosie's test

and you knew you'd have to tell him why.

Then again, that Christmas vacation when
you were playing Careers and you hurt Tate
because you were so angry and then so

ashamed. And, finally, in February
in the rink, watching your brothers' game, when
you thought about either getting your period
or an abortion and having to talk
to Mum about it and then to Daddy.

It ran up through your body with such calm,
reasonably, telling you to leave,
to quit – a funnel opened in your middle,
air pushed past your skin – a hallowed stillness,

knowing this you could now do.

You'd both been disappointed. Maybe you'd
both dreamed the moment much too much. Yours
had not been easily given. Next time, you'd tried
two times before finally giving up, falling
asleep, Tate crying without making sound.

Golden Rod

The water off the light
bounces, scoops, and rolls,
a conversation between

elements, as elemental as
your aloneness which cannot be
altered no matter how

many thoughts with which you've filled
your head, standing at the sink,
sipping tea, watching

the pond at play.
Along its shores, the golden rod's
yellow fingers turn summer's

final page, while upstairs
Weezie could be emptying
everything all over again.

Time Telling

Her leave of absence – not
here, there or anywhere
for now, now being

what it is – you remember
trying to teach Weezie
about the minute hand tipping

into the next hour, hour
hand into the next day, days
into week, weeks into

years – how she begged you
to stop. Today she won't
even let you touch her.

You can sit beside her only,
she asks, if you don't
breathe too loudly.

Since she was born, the truth is,
you've had all these little choices,
and love has made them

bearable – a ship you sail
upon as you are pulled
together toward all time.

Not Vast but Wilderness

You wonder if you've had a right to rage
and fear – all those novels you read giving
you an attic to contain them. Perhaps,
after all, this story will be about
all of you – how you might have eased each
other's pain, been more joyful. No matter
what he said, it wasn't good enough, Tate
told you.

                You had such differences to choose
between – theirs and his. Some days you felt dead
before you were dead, laying your head in
every place, staying awake, and watching
light exchange its place with dark.

                                  Not
vast but wilderness to you, you beat your
way through your past.

                        You always did apologize –
something at which, Mum would say, you were so

very good.

Ho Jo and Flo

Flo was fifty-six and you were eighteen.
Flo lived on Cedar Street, and you slept on
a day bed in her front room with your head
next to the door that led to the stairs which
led to the street. Flo was terrified of
her fellow man. "Take your name tag off when
you walk home," she whimpered. But you loved
everyone – the two ladies who complained
their frappes tasted like water, the guy who
sold you white shoes and refused to tax you,
the boy who read your name tag on the Common
and said, "Hi!" She'd been Mum's nanny, Pop's ward,
and had lived alone and worked ever since
as a secretary at Shreve, Crump and Low.

You'd get home from work and take a shower.
When you sat down to supper, she'd say, "You
must be clean inside and out." Then when Tate
came to pick you up at ten thirty at
night after his rehearsal to go to
his grandmother's, Flo would call you into
her room and tell you she thought you were being
inconsiderate – her sharp little intake
of air, then silence. So, at lunch one day
when an elderly woman came in and
you didn't notice her until the hostess
pointed her out to you, saying she had
already given her a glass of wine,
and after you finally attended
to her, off a three-dollar check, she tipped
you a dollar, you held her hand and smiled.
Most of the people who worked there hated

your guts. The cooks mimicked you in falsetto
when you asked for toast on your plates. You overheard
one of them saying, "I'm sick and tired of this
sweet and innocent stuff. I don't buy it
anymore." So, you really didn't want
anyone to know why you were crying
after Daddy called on the pay phone one
afternoon to say you'd gotten in off
the waiting list, for the same reason you didn't
want anyone to know Pop was the lawyer
for Howard Johnson and he'd gotten you
the job, but when Athena, the middle-aged Greek
waitress who had trained you on your first days,
came to you about the things the cooks were calling
her, you two sat in a back booth with Tina
and smoked cigarettes, and you ended up
telling both of them. That's when Tina made
you swear you wouldn't tell anyone her
legal name was Timothy and she'd been
saving her money for an operation.

By then you'd have only six more days till
Tate would help you move your day bed out of
Flo's and you'd punch out of Ho Jo's for the
last time. You and Flo would be having wine
with your dinners; you'd always share break with
Tina and Athena and smoke each other's
cigarettes, and you and Athena would
cover for Tina when she had to take
emergency breaks to adjust some things,
and on your final day, you'd give a homeless
man fifty cents for a cup of coffee,
and he would bow to kiss your helpful hand.

Won't You Be

Tate told you he didn't know
what he was doing with you anymore or why
you were there at his grandmother's
one week before college began.

But you knew. You were lying
in bed beside him, listening
to the waves hit

the sand, then hit it again, again,
again, and you were watching
the light hit the leaves
of the tree outside the window,

while below you, his grandmother, who was
deaf and a little blind and too old
to climb the stairs, started frying bacon.

The night before, she'd said she hoped
she wouldn't here
in the morning. She said that

every night. You didn't call home,
didn't start to pack, didn't tell them when
you'd be back, didn't
want them to know.

When Tate woke up,
you brushed your teeth together,
singing, "It's a beautiful
day in the neighborhood."

Fly Away Home

Your brothers, grown men now,
with families of their own, gather
in the hall as Mum hands you all

your gifts, which she asked of you,
fearing she would never have enough –
her mouth stitched in the lines

of its own pursing, hair white and wild,
standing around her head, as if it, too,
would never eat all that,

the eldest of your brothers smiling
sadly, just behind, and Daddy somewhere
else, where only he could be. Before,

as you were packing up your car
beneath a flock of blue
birds beating branch to branch

within the wintry trees, your brother
told you what he'd only just discovered –
a visceral response to your latest

departure – that all this love
that he'd once known was leaving –
from a boy, your going first,

while the rest of them would stay.

Sonnet for Freshman English

Tate let you read the one he wrote. It was
about how you could not seem to say
"thank you," ruled the relationship because
your standards were so high, about the way

Tate felt he had to try to measure up
to them, about your loving him in spite
of himself. Of course, you knew you loved him, but
whenever he asked you to say the reason why,

you couldn't seem to utter a response.
Before he showed you a letter Sarah sent,
he tried to warn you, "Give her thoughts a chance."
You'd like to say you tried, but you could not –

She's bad for you. Why can't you see it, Tate?
If you don't get out now, you'll only come to hate.

Between the Window and the Door

You write what you write,
what has not been obvious to you.

You think you think
these things all by yourself?

When you read your journals,
you find some thoughts you won't

repeat – blame is another solitude
that stands up straight between

the window and the door, keeping
its secrets, spiteful and afraid.

You were a helpless girl
no one could help. Now

there's a thought that might return
to eat from both your hands.

Not as Much

When it was two weeks since you'd last heard from
him, and you were reconciled and ready
the phone rang, and it was Tate saying, "It's
me." You could have pretended not to know
whose voice it was, wishing you weren't so
single-hearted, were more like other girls
who slept with other boys, carrying their
affections around on a tray as if
they were appetizers, hardly filling,
not killing the buzz. He'd already

asked you if you'd break up with him because
of a girl named Cindi. You were trying
to quit cigarettes, trying to lose weight,
trying out for Juliet and almost
getting cast opposite him. After

reading two more tales for next week's Chaucer
exam, you changed your mind and called him back
to be greeted by a reluctant "okay."
You arrived in his room and found yourself
sitting on a note from Cindi who dotted
her "I's" with little hearts. After he left
for a rehearsal, you opened it and

read what it said. The first time Tate kissed you
four years ago, he sang, "I love you more
today than yesterday." You fell asleep,
alone in his bed, woke up beside him
again; got shin splints running, late for class.

Shbag

It turns out understanding's not
required. All that's necessary is
a giving up, a letting go – surrender
and cessation and a promise of
relief from your own corrosive rage.

No more resentment, no need to
forget, regardless of how well-
deserved – a gift unto yourself –

merciful and measured, as old-
fashioned as Daddy's prayers,
as eloquent as evening closing

out another day. Will love be
reason enough? You'll not have
considered it excuse before –
all anyone has to plead a cause
justly or unjustly. No thing is

perfect except in how you see it and
in the words you use to tell about it –

remission, pardon, absolution,
indulgence, clemency, reprieve,
exoneration, dispensation, amnesty.

Saturday, After Midnight

His knock was faint, but you woke to let
him in. You must've been waiting. You'd been
thinking about him all summer. You got
the two of you some scotch. He sat on

Sarah's bed. You got back in yours, the room,
which had been empty for the weekend, now
full, Rosie and Sarah out with boys somewhere
elsewhere. You finished the bottle. You kept

most of the room between you like that until
he had to pee, and when he came back, he
sat beside you and asked how you felt with
him so close. That was when you got up and

fetched the post card you had never mailed, asking
him how he was because you couldn't seem
to get in touch with him. And then you were
kissing without stopping. Later, as you

lay beside him, you watched the line of dark
between the rooftops and the bottom of
the shade. You thought a lot but mostly about
not thinking, not being able to think. At

one point you got up to pee and before
coming back to bed, you stood at the window,
looking out across the campus – lecture hall,
library, and gym – and thought something

definitive and comforting, but then forgot
what that thought was. When you got back in bed,

he was awake. You can't remember what
he said, but finally you fell asleep

until just before the alarm went off.
He took forever to wake up, dozing off
as he had always done. You lay there thinking
what you had and hadn't been thinking before,

and while you were busy thinking all the right
things, Tate woke up enough to say not to let
this make you unhappy, and then you did
the wrong thing and rolled on top of him again.

No Cause, No Cause

Lying on the study floor with your
little brothers watching the Red Sox,
eating leftover spaghetti for
breakfast with Mum before church; the night
you both slept in the yard because your
parents were away and you'd made a
promise; running to his dorm, to class,
to and from each other – you had to
keep teaching each other how. All you

were doing was missing everything you missed,
drinking coffee, skipping class, reading
King Lear at the Woolworth's lunch counter –
Cordelia in the last scenes; hoping
to be found, dreaming of being sought.

You were the only one who took yourself
so seriously. Maybe it was time to stop.

Baby Teeth

In the bottom of Pop's old dresser-top box,
their jagged ends unrooted, like broken

pearls no one would wear, all Weezie's
baby teeth hide where you tucked them,
one after the other each time she lost,

and you – what did you lose?

One day she will open this box, here now
on your dresser, after she has lost
an earring or a hair clip

or you, perhaps, and she will wonder,
Why these small and useless bones?

And you might no longer be
available to explain.

Using Your Words

Sitting in a toilet stall at Head Start,
waiting for Colin to tinkle in the
potty, sometimes you wondered was this all
you were prepared for, likely to
be good at. The day before, Colin had
pointed at the tank where, the day before
that, there had been two fish, and now there was
only one. "What happened to the other
fish, Colin? Tell me using your words."

"It's missing, Miss," he said.

Lately you'd been rethinking the pleasures
of solitude. You felt things all the time –
too much – and you tried to match the weight of
your feelings to the height of your thoughts.

Sometimes you wanted to spend your final
semesters of college way up in the
observation tower of the John Hancock,
wandering around and around while a

tiny world crawled far below. Sometimes you
wanted to plunge into the rushing crowds
and rush around with them, especially
at night. You wanted to know what you were
and then never to think of it again.

Being Pleased

Not sure
what has kept you,

made you
stay, you

always got lost,
never got found,

didn't really know
where you were

most of the time,
even as you were

exactly where
you'd almost always

been. You
wonder who was

standing in
those bones,

who was being
pleased.

The Various Shapes of Leaves

Under her bed, a box of notebooks
Weezie left behind reminds you how she's
always gathered up her words. Sometimes you'd
find them on receipts or napkins, a paper
cup – *hemlock-heavy horizon, score the
shore, fake mistake, the longest wrongest where*

I belongest. Randall drives past her
apartment at least twice a day, eats lunch
at the diner across from the music
shop where she works. The bed of his truck fills
with leaves that fall from the trees. He lowers
the tail gate so when he drives back to the
job site, they dance around his box of tools,
faster and faster until they fly away.

He taught her how to drive as soon as her
feet could reach the clutch, to name the birds, the clouds,
the rocks, bugs, stars and trees, especially

the trees – the textures of their bark, the heights
of every canopy, the various shapes of leaves.

Becoming

Sarah walked around the room, repeating,
"We are twenty. Almost twenty-one. I'm

so sorry. That's so scary." When you watched
the news, she went off on Governor King
wanting to reinstate capital
punishment and refusing to fund
abortions for rape victims. Meanwhile
Rosie would be saying, "Oh, just don't think
about it." or "I just want to live my
life out until I die without any
complications." As usual, they'd change
the channel to *Courtship of Eddie's Father*
and decide to eat ice cream. As usual,
you were trying to quit cigarettes
but ended up smoking three before bed
and got frightened when you woke up and
had trouble breathing. The more you promised

yourself to stop, the more you stuffed yourself.
It was either eat or smoke or talk and
be so nervous. Mum said, none of which was
becoming. You just had to stop eating.
You had to. You had to. You had to. You
sat with Sarah and Rosie and noticed
you imitated one then the other
alternately, and so you fell silent

and suddenly were, again, yourself. You'd

always had to work so hard to get a part
down before performance – hours in
front of a mirror, becoming somebody
else's idea of somebody else.

Unbecoming

No desserts. No butter,
peanut or otherwise.

No dressings on salads.
No starches. No granola.

1 spoonful honey per day.
8 glasses water.

1 spoonful lecithin.
5 spoonfuls bran.
1 spoonful brewer's yeast.

No breakfast – just slows you down.
Lunch – one piece of fruit.
Dinner – yogurt, cottage cheese, bran,
lecithin, brewer's yeast.
Beverages – black tea, black coffee, water.

Weight: one hundred and twenty-three.
Goal: lose ten pounds (and still weigh ten
pounds more than you did six months ago).

The Forgiveness Bowl

Just after Weezie was born, Mum gave you
a bowl she made at one of those paint your
own pottery places – dark purple with
flowers along the rim. "We were too hard
on you," she said. "You were our only daughter."

What choices did you have except yourselves
and each other? Did anything else matter?

You can only be as full as you are
empty, as here as you were ever there.

Some love you choose. Some love chooses you. Call
it love or wish it love, when what you mean
is something else – a knot you must untie.

Learning How to Tie

"The rabbit goes round the tree and through
the hole and snugs in tight."

Your brothers leaned against you, learning longer than
was necessary, loving your loving

them, while Weezie whispered all the words, wound the knot,
went away, wanting what

you never knew. Will time afford you answers? Or does it
simply untie possibilities,

loosening their grip upon the truth
that time is not a line at all, but loops that double back

around and through, swooping into memory, then out again –
all that matters – the past encircling

the future, each beginning in each ending. Like the moon
which fills and empties with the light

of other planets, you raised a daughter of your own,
and though you dig earth

to find water, dive water to find rock, great love is absence,
beyond containment from the moment

she was born. Beware
the beggar in disguise.

See how the birds sipping seeds in empty fields
are loving nothing.

Burden of the Past

Such high expectations for years and years, and, always,
you fell short of them – you've re-read what you wrote,

recognized you were doing your best – a familiar girl,
difficult, unmeasured; everyone was. Half finished

reading Jackson Bate's book on Johnson for your last exam,
exhausted but couldn't sleep, you suddenly decided

to walk all over town, looking for another notebook,
which you found at Store 24, and a pen. Bate made

you believe you have conviction, and his affection
drove you round the corner, down the street,

back up the dormitory stairs and to your room.
There will always be something to say.

Blue Flight, Blue Bird, Sky

One more bow taken, your face
the only word no script
could replace, the curtain
fell, spotlight faded on unasked
questions you've still no
answers to, though love,
with its knapsack of redemptions,
came knocking again.

Who was there?

Randall, when first he held
Weezie, sang *You have captured
me. I can't get free* – the blue

flight of the blue
bird, a reminder
of the sky.

At Its Best

Your feet eventually not touching the
sandy bottom, waves at your ribs, then armpits,
shoulders, chin – your desperate scanning of
the beach – Mum was nowhere in sight, way back
where the water first took you from her.
You thought then, for the first time, you would die,
until a stranger took your hand and walked
you in to shore. Without a word, you ran
back to your towel, your brothers, your mother
who never knew what she had almost lost.
You didn't ever tell her, standing in
your trembling body, your baby teeth
clattering as she handed you a peanut
butter and jelly sandwich crisp with sun.

"Water doesn't lie," Randall kept saying
this past winter when the ice dams almost
ruined your house, finding every crack
and flaw in workmanship with which your house
was built. Gutters jammed. Window wells filled. From
the eaves, long clear fingers pointed at
the easiest way down, and the walls were
stained with leavings.

                    At its best, love might
tell us who we are, but the elements
are guaranteed to put us in our place.
Above all, the stars, which appear to be
constant, have died so very long ago.

Housekeeping

As do the common sparrows
nesting out your door, Mum
brought back up what she had

swallowed, spewed it down
your throat, then took between
her teeth the offal you expressed.

You wonder if the birds ingest
the waste – a waste or not?
Every insult, injury, complaint.

So, nothing would get lost, be
gone, and all that's thus transformed
would be completely given.

Each of you has what the other
would take back if only time
and truth allowed. Often,

you haven't meant exactly
what you've said, and Weezie
has to have heard. Oh, how a word

can fail to fly away once it has spread
its wings, lingering in its crowded
nest, fearful of both sky and ground.

Having It All

Even in your happy house,
rage hid behind the door,
surprising you so suddenly,
you slammed and broke and roared.

It held your breath and squeezed you
tight and then you were released.
You looked around without a sound
at all that you'd unleashed.

The whisper of your baby's hands
upon your collarbones
restored the time, the truth, the shame.
No longer had you else to blame.

You set the pot back on the stove,
wiped your tears, apologized,
hoped this love enough to bear,
was strong and good and wise.

In years that come, you've learned to step
aside when anger's shrill,
allowed it space to sit and glare
until it's had its fill,

to talk to it in soothing tones,
to feed it from the same
dishes you serve all your guests,
to recognize and say its name.

The Knot

Regardless of what you
have done and what
you have not done,

as Louisiana has grown up,
you have been waiting
for her to become

enough, using your words,
which rarely do
the same thing

twice, though you've tried
to catch and tame them,
lock them up

and name them.
You've had to learn
to let them

go and hope,
if they return,
they'll eat from both

your hands.

The Rest of It

As time tiptoes
from room to room,
leaving doors

ajar, you are still
busy learning where
all your days are –

revolving light,
then night, day after
day – those firsts,

these lasts – the rest
of it. The rough-winged
sparrows are plentiful

this spring. If you hold
still, you will
hear them fly.

The Dragonfly

The dragonfly settles its green and black wings –
one set of feet on *always*, the other on *about to* –
the sentence you were writing as you searched for ways
to tame what has become. You hope you are
a story to tell that is really about everyone else.

What words you'll have to use to get it right.

Something about silence is safe, but a voice
is also what is given – how to strike a balance,
be patient, make mistakes and recover, not to stop.

Daddy always loved Mum for her sense of outrage,
and with Weezie, who only tried to please, you made
your own little bargains, but maybe you don't know
anything about them beyond the parts to do

with you. Louisiana calls to say she's found love
again, and you have started to understand all else
love can be, its sufferings – its excesses – the bowls
of its fruit. Forgive it. It has been plenty, and enough.

Unhitch it from its useless names. Let them beat
their glassy wings, those ancient bones, arise again.

Your house is not burning.
Hold tight to each turning.
There will be no perfect

anything – warm beds,
full plates, boots by the back door,
key where we'll always
know to find it.

About the Author

Laura Rogerson Moore has lived and worked in Groton, Massachusetts, for most of her life. In 2010, Finishing Line Press published her chapbook *Yahoodips*.

www.ingramcontent.com/pod-product-compliance
Lightning Source LLC
LaVergne TN
LVHW020100090426
835510LV00040B/2669